THE OLYMPICS
RECORDS

THE OLYMPICS
RECORDS

Moira Butterfield

SEA-TO-SEA
Mankato Collingwood London

This edition first published in 2012 by

Sea-to-Sea Publications
Distributed by Black Rabbit Books
P.O. Box 3263, Mankato, Minnesota 56002

Printed in United States of America, North Mankato, MN

9 8 7 6 5 4 3

Published by arrangement with the Watts
Publishing Group Ltd, London.

Library of Congress Cataloging-in-Publication Data

Butterfield, Moira, 1960-
  The Olympics: Records / by Moira Butterfield.
     p. cm. -- (The Olympics)
  Includes index.
  ISBN 978-1-59771-322-1 (library binding)
  1. Olympics--Records--Juvenile literature. I. Title.
  GV721.8.B88 2012
  796.48--dc22
                                    2011006471

Series editor: Sarah Ridley
Editor in chief: John C. Miles
Designer: Jason Billin
Art director: Jonathan Hair
Picture research: Diana Morris

Picture credits: Robert Beck/Sports Illustrated/Getty Images: 29. Al Bello/Getty Images: 20b.
Lutz Bongarts/Getty Images: 19c. Simon Bruty/Sports Illustrated/Getty Images: 25. Martin
Bureau/AFP/Getty Images: 6. Nat Farbman/Time & Life Pictures/Getty Images: 16. Bill Frakes/Sports
Illustrated/Getty Images: 8. Getty Images: 10t, 23. Jeff Haynes/AFP/Getty Images: 7. Image
Works/Topfoto: 26. IOC/Allsport/Getty Images: 9t. Lynn Johnson/Sports Illustrated/Getty Images: 15t.
Li Ga/Xinhua/Newsteam International: front cover, 13. Bob Martin/Allsport/Getty Images: 11. Douglas
Miller/Hulton Archive/Getty Images: 12. Picturepoint/Topham: 22. Mike Powell/Allsport/Getty Images:
3, 10b, 19t, 28. Steve Powell/Allsport/Getty Images: 9c. Robert Riger/Getty Images: 17. George
Silk/Time & Life Pictures/Getty Images: 24. Michael Steele/Allsport/Getty Images: 14, 15c. Matthew
Stockman/Getty Images: 27. Ullsteinbild/Topfoto: 5, 21t, 21c. Koji Watanabe/Getty Images: 18.
xia ming/CC./Wikimedia Commons/20c.

November 2011
RD/9781597712910/002

Note to parents and teachers

Every effort has been made by the Publishers to ensure that the web sites in this book
are suitable for children, that they are of the highest educational value, and that they
contain no inappropriate or offensive material. However, because of the nature of the
Internet, it is impossible to guarantee that the contents of these sites will not be altered.
We strongly advise that Internet access is supervised by a responsible adult.

CONTENTS

RECORDS

An Olympic record is a best performance ever in an Olympic Games. It could be a fastest time, a highest score, or a record number of medals. The world's greatest sportsmen and women have set incredible Olympic records since the modern Olympic Games began in 1896.

Olympic record performances are measured and confirmed by the International Olympic Committee (the IOC). Hundreds of technicians work at each Games overseeing electronic timing devices set up at finish lines. The timing devices stretch an invisible light beam across the finish and measure when the beam is broken, pinpointing the time in hundredths of a second. There are also electronic photo-finish cameras. In the Olympic swimming pool, electronic touchpads at the end of each lane automatically record the time when swimmers touch them.

◀ These judges, seated by the Olympic pool, are ready to score a swimming event.

Judging Olympic Sports

In some Olympic sports, performances are not timed. Instead they are given scores by a team of judges. Summer sports such as gymnastics, dressage, diving, boxing, and synchronized swimming are scored this way, along with some winter sports. Because this type of scoring is based on personal opinion, it has often led to arguments or protests.

Disqualifications

Olympic records are canceled if athletes are caught cheating by taking performance-enhancing drugs. In 1988, Canadian Ben Johnson broke the record for running the men's 100 meters (m), but when he was disqualified for taking drugs, the record was canceled. When American athlete Marion Jones admitted taking drugs, she was stripped of the five medals she had won at the Sydney Games in 2000, and her name was wiped from the record books.

Officials check equipment on the Olympic track.

Amazing Olympics

An Olympic record might not be the same as a world record, if the world record was set at a different event outside the Games.

Olympic Facts and Stats

American swimmer Michael Phelps has won a record 16 Olympic medals, 14 of them gold (see page 20).

American Paralympic swimmer Trischa Zorn has won an incredible record-breaking 55 medals, 41 of them gold (see page 26). Her total is more than double that of any other Paralympic athlete.

The first modern Olympic record ever was set at the first modern Olympics, held in 1896. The first race was a heat of the men's 100 m, and it was won by American runner Francis Lane in 12.2 seconds.

Some sports, such as the standing jump, have been dropped from the Olympics over the years, so their final Olympic records will never be beaten.

FASTEST MEN EVER

Olympic track events are races that take place on the athletics track in the main Olympic Stadium. They showcase the world's fastest athletes.

Sprints are the fastest running races in the Olympics—the 100 m, 200 m, and 400 m races—and the winning sprinters become big stars. The world's fastest man, Jamaican Usain Bolt, set an incredible Olympic record for the 100 m of 9.69 seconds at Beijing in 2008. He has run faster since then, outside the Olympics. At Beijing, he also smashed the Olympic 200 m record and helped his team to a record 4 x 100 m relay victory.

Usain Bolt, 2008 Olympic champion of the 100 m and 200 m sprint races.

Amazing Olympics

The first Olympic Games ever were held in ancient Greece around 776 B.C.E. and had only one event, called the Stadion—a men's sprint of 210 yards (192.2 m).

▶ Paavo Nurmi of Finland, a middle-distance runner, won three gold medals in 1920 and five more in 1924.

Middle- and Long-Distance Races

Middle- and long-distance track races include the 800 m, 1,500 m, 3,000 m, 5,000 m, and 10,000 m. One of the greatest middle-distance Olympic athletes of all time was Paavo Nurmi, nicknamed "The Flying Finn." Another Finnish long-distance running hero was Lasse Virén, who fell during the 10,000 m race in 1972 but still won in record time. Great Britain's Sebastian Coe won four Olympic medals, including the 1,500 m gold medal at the Olympic Games in 1980 and 1984, and set eight outdoor and three indoor world records.

▶ Sebastian Coe won four Olympic medals and held eight world records during his career.

Olympic Facts and Stats——Fastest Olympic Men

100 m sprint—Usain Bolt—Jamaica—9.69 secs—Beijing 2008

200 m sprint—Usain Bolt—Jamaica—19.3 secs—Beijing 2008

400 m sprint—Michael Johnson—USA—43.49—Atlanta 1996

400 m hurdles—Kevin Young—USA—46.78—Barcelona 1992

1,500 m run—Noah Ngeny—Kenya—3:32.07—Sydney 2000

10,000 m run—Kenenisa Bekele—Ethiopia—27:01.17—Beijing 2008

Cycling sprint—Chris Hoy—GB—9.815 seconds—Beijing 2008

500 m speed skating—Casey FitzRandolph—USA—34.42 seconds (average speed 32.5 mph [52.37 km/h])—Salt Lake City 2002

For the first few years of the modern Olympics, women were not allowed to compete in track events because running was thought too dangerous and unladylike. They were finally allowed to race in 1928.

Fanny Blankers-Koen of the Netherlands is regarded by many as the greatest female sprinter ever. At the 1948 Games she won four gold medals—the 100 m, 200 m, 800 m, and 4 x 100 m relay.

Fanny Blankers-Koen (Netherlands), one of the greatest female Olympic sprinters ever.

American athlete Florence Griffith Joyner, nicknamed Flo-Jo, holds the Olympic record for the 100 m and the 200 m. She also holds the 100 m world record at 10.49 seconds, which she set in an Olympic trial event. She was famous for her looks as well as her running because she wore unusual running clothes. She won three gold and two silver medals in the 1984 and 1988 Olympics.

American sprinter Florence Griffith Joyner, the women's world record holder for the 100 m and 200 m.

Middle- and Long-Distance Races

In 1928 some female athletes collapsed with exhaustion after the 800 m. Even though male athletes did the same, the IOC decided it was too dangerous for women to run middle- or long-distance races and the events were only allowed back into the Olympics in 1960. In a historic 10,000 m final in Barcelona in 1992, Ethiopia's Derartu Tulu became the first black African female Olympic medalist ever. Since then African women athletes, especially those from Ethiopia and Kenya, have set records and won many medals.

Recent Records

Few women's sprinting records have been broken in the last 20 years, and it's thought that this could be partly due to athletes taking performance-enhancing drugs in previous decades, before tests were as thorough as they are now.

▶ Ethiopia's Derartu Tulu, the first black African female Olympic gold medalist ever. She won long-distance running golds in 1992 and 2000.

Olympic Facts and Stats——Fastest Olympic Women

100 m sprint—Florence Griffith Joyner—USA—10.62 seconds—Seoul 1988

200 m sprint—Florence Griffith Joyner—USA—21.34 seconds—Seoul 1988

400 m sprint—Marie-Jose Perec—France—48.25 seconds—Atlanta 1996

800 m sprint—Nadezhda Olizarenko—USSR—1:53.43—Moscow 1980

100 m hurdles—Joanna Hayes—USA—12.37 seconds—Athens 2004

Cycling sprint—Victoria Pendleton—GB—10.963—Beijing 2008

500 m speed skating—Catriona LeMay Doan—Canada—37.3 seconds
(average speed 30 mph [48.26 km/h])—Salt Lake City 2002

HIGHEST AND LONGEST

Field events are held in the middle of the main stadium at the Summer Olympics. They have produced many remarkable sports heroes in events such as high jump and long jump, and in throwing events including the javelin.

In 1936, American athlete and four-times gold medalist Jesse Owens set a world long-jump record that no one broke for an amazing 25 years. American long jumper Bob Beamon finally smashed it at the Mexico Olympics in 1968, and his achievement still stands as an Olympic record. After the jump, he collapsed in shock at what he had achieved, and because the jump was so long, the judges had to find an extra measuring tape to find out how far he'd jumped. Fellow American Carl Lewis won long-jump gold at the Barcelona Olympics in 1992 and became one of the true Olympic greats, winning ten Olympic medals, nine of them gold, for sprinting and long jump.

◀ American athlete Bob Beamon finally smashed a long-jump record that had remained unbroken for 25 years.

Amazing Olympics

The standing jump (a high jump with no running start) was won eight times by American Ray Ewry, nicknamed "the human frog." It is no longer an Olympic event.

High Jump and Pole Vault

Records are sometimes broken when new techniques or equipment are introduced. At the 1968 Olympics, American high jumper Dick Fosbury won the gold medal and set an Olympic record with a new type of jump he had invented, called the "Fosbury flop." Now most high jumpers use this jump. Meanwhile, Olympic pole vaulters were able to reach new heights when fiberglass poles replaced bamboo ones. Russian Olympic pole-vault superstar Yelena Isinbayeva has so far won two gold medals, and broken more than 27 world records in her career.

Discus and Javelin

Discus and javelin events date back to the ancient Olympics. Czech Jan Zelezny is the most successful Olympic javelin star. He won three gold medals and a silver between 1992 and 2000. One of the greatest sportswomen ever, Babe Didrikson, won javelin gold for the USA in 1932.

▶ Russian Olympic gold medalist Yelena Isinbayeva has broken many world records in her pole-vaulting career.

Olympic Facts and Stats

Men's high jump—Charles Austin—USA—7.84 ft. (2.39 m)—Atlanta 1996
Women's high jump—Yelena Slesarenko—Russian Federation—6.75 ft. (2.06 m)—Athens 2004
Men's pole vault—Steven Hooker—Australia—19.55 ft. (5.96 m)—Beijing 2008
Women's pole vault—Yelena Isinbayeva—Russia—16.56 ft. (5.05 m)—Beijing 2008
Men's long jump—Bob Beamon—USA—29.19 ft. (8.9 m)—Mexico City 1968
Women's long jump—Jackie Joyner-Kersee—USA—24.27 ft. (7.4 m)—Seoul 1988
Men's triple jump—Kenny Harrison—USA—59.35 ft. (18.09 m)—Atlanta 1996
Women's triple jump—Francoise Mbango Etone—Cameroon—50.5 ft. (15.39 m)—Beijing 2008
Men's javelin—Andreas Thorkildsen—Norway—297.14 ft. (90.57 m)—Beijing 2008
Women's javelin—Osleidys Menendez—234.67 ft. (71.53 m)—Athens 2004

Olympic sports such as weightlifting, hammer-throwing, and shot put need feats of super strength as well as good technique to achieve records.

Olympic weightlifters lift a barbell loaded with weight plates. There are different categories based on the bodyweight of contestants, from the smallest "bantam" weightlifters to the "super-heavyweights," the world's strongest men and women. The 1948 bantamweight men's gold medalist, Joe De Pietro, was so short he could only just get the barbell above his head. The most successful super-heavyweight star was Iranian weightlifter Hosséin Rezazadeh, nicknamed "the Iranian Hercules." He won two Olympic gold medals in 2000 and 2004, as well as many world championships, and he became so famous in Iran that his wedding was broadcast on live TV.

Amazing Olympics

Olympic throwing events once included stone-throwing and throwing a 56-lb. (25.4-kg) weight.

Hosséin Rezazadeh, Iranian superstar weightlifter, won two Olympic golds in 2000 and 2004.

Women's Weightlifting

Women's weightlifting began in Sydney in 2000 and it has since produced some ground-breaking new female champions. "Flyweight" Nurcan Taylan was the first Turkish woman ever to win an Olympic gold medal. "Featherweight" Udomporn Polsak became the first Thai woman ever to win an Olympic gold, and "light heavyweight" bronze-medalist Karnam Malleswari became the first Indian woman ever to win an Olympic medal of any kind. They were all heroines back home.

△ Nurcan Taylan, Turkish Olympic gold medalist in the female flyweight competition.

The Throwers

Hammer-throwing heroes include American athlete Matt McGrath, who won two gold and silver medals, and set an Olympic record in 1912 that lasted 24 years. In 2000, when Finn Arsi Harju won a gold for the shotput, the people in his hometown gave him a Harley-Davidson motorcycle because they couldn't afford the traditional Finnish reward of a house or plot of land.

◁ Finnish shotput star Arsi Harju won Olympic gold in 2000.

Olympic Facts and Stats

Men's shotput—Ulf Timmermann—East Germany 73.72 ft. (22.47 m)—Seoul 1988

Men's hammer—Sergey Litvinov—USSR—278.2 ft. (84.8 m)—Seoul 1988

Women's shot put—Ilona Slupianek—East Germany—73.52 ft. (22.41 m)—Moscow 1980

Women's hammer—Aksana Miankova—Belarus—250.459 ft. (76.34 m)—Beijing 2008

Men's weightlifting 105 kg+ class—Hosséin Rezazadeh—Iran—Combined Snatch and Clean and Jerk weight—1,041.68 lb. (472.5 kg)—Sydney 2000

Women's weightlifting 75 kg+ class—Jang Mi-Ran—South Korea—Combined Snatch and Clean and Jerk weight—718.7 lb. (326 kg)—Beijing 2008

Some Olympic events take a lot of stamina over long periods of time. Athletes taking part in the marathon, the decathlon, and long-distance cycling and swimming must keep up their performance for hours to break records and win medals.

The first Olympic marathon was run in 1896 in Greece, and was won by a Greek shepherd named Spiridon Louis, who became a national hero. In 1952, Czech star Emil Zatopek set a men's Olympic marathon record of 2 hours 23 minutes 3.2 seconds, a record that lasted until 1976. Zatopek ran the 5,000 m and the 10,000 m later the same week, winning all of them. Like the marathon, the Olympic 50,000 m walk is held mainly on roads outside the stadium. Pole Robert Korzeniowski has a world-beating four gold medals for walking.

Amazing Olympics

A brand new long-distance swimming event, the 10,000 m marathon, was introduced in 2008. It is swum outdoors in open water.

◀ Czech long-distance running maestro Emil Zatopek won four Olympic gold medals.

Combined Events

The men's decathlon is made up of ten different events held over two days, and athletes build up a points total. Daley Thompson of Great Britain won two decathlon gold medals in 1980 and 1984. Women compete in the seven-event heptathlon and the five-event modern pentathlon.

Cycling Endurance Events

Olympic long-distance cyclists encounter extreme heat, collisions, falls, and even protestors along the roads of the host nation. There are no Olympic records in long-distance cycling because the courses are different at each Olympics. The most successful Olympic road-racing cyclist is Dutch woman Leontien Zijlaard-van Moorsel, with four golds.

○ American star Jackie Joyner-Kersee (right) was the first heptathlete ever to score more than 7,000 points. She won two Olympic golds in the event.

Olympic Facts and Stats

Men's marathon—Samuel Wanjiru—Kenya—2 hours 6 minutes 32 seconds—Beijing 2008

Women's marathon—Naoko Takahashi—Japan—2 hours 23 minutes 14 seconds—Sydney 2000

Marathon 10 km swim (men)—Maarten van der Weijden—Netherlands—1 hour 51 minutes 51 seconds -- Beijing 2008

Marathon 10 km swim (women)—Larisa Ilchenko—Russia—2 hours 19 minutes 49 seconds—Beijing 2008

Decathlon (men-only event)—Roman Sebrle—Czech Republic—8,893 points—Athens 2004

Heptathlon (women-only event)—Jackie Joyner-Kersee—USA—7,291 points—Seoul 1988

50,000 m walk (men-only event)—Alex Schwazer—Italy—3 hours 37 minutes 9 seconds—Beijing 2008

TEAM SPORTS

Olympic team sports records are measured by a high number of gold medals or very high scores. Summer Olympic team events include soccer, basketball, volleyball, handball, hockey, rowing, and team cycling.

Remarkable Olympic team performances include the Indian men's hockey team, which won six gold medals in a row between 1928 and 1956. Their most famous goal-scoring hero was Dhyan Chand, regarded as one of the greatest hockey players ever. The Hungarian team won a record seven gold medals in a row for team saber fencing between 1928 and 1960, and they have won a record ten gold medals overall.

Basketball
The most successful Olympic team ever is the American men's basketball team, which has won 13 gold medals. Professionals—people who earn money from their sport—have been allowed in the Olympics

The American women's Olympic soccer team celebrating a third gold medal in 2008.

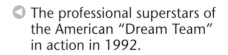

The professional superstars of the American "Dream Team" in action in 1992.

since 1988, and the change of rules led to the basketball team being made up of professional superstars. The 1992 team was nicknamed the "Dream Team" because it contained basketball stars such as Michael Jordan and Magic Johnson.

Team Rowing

Olympic team rowing events have produced two great British Olympians. Steve Redgrave won five gold medals in a row from 1984 to 2000, for the coxed four and the coxless pair teams. His rowing colleague Matthew Pinsent won four gold medals in a row. Both men were knighted by the Queen after their run of medal successes.

Gold for the Great Britain coxless four rowing team in 2000, including Steve Redgrave and Matthew Pinsent.

Amazing Olympics

The team sport of rugby sevens will be introduced at the 2016 Olympic Games in Rio de Janeiro.

Olympic Facts and Stats

Best Olympic basketball performance—the 1956 American men's basketball team won every game they played by at least 30 points.

Best Winter Olympics team—the Canadian ice-hockey team has won ten gold medals.

Best Olympic men's soccer team—Hungary, with three gold medals, a silver, and a bronze.

Best Olympic women's soccer team—USA, with three gold medals.

Highest-scoring Olympic soccer game—1912—Denmark 17, France 1. Sophus Nielsen of Denmark scored ten of the goals.

WATER GOLDS

Some of the biggest Olympic medal hauls ever have been won in or on the water, in the Olympic swimming pool or out on the kayak and sailing courses.

American swimmer Michael Phelps won eight gold medals in Beijing in 2008, a record for one Games. His total number of gold medals is 14, making him the most successful Olympic competitor ever, in any sport. Nicknamed the "Baltimore Bullet," he kept his strength up at the Beijing Olympics by eating record-breaking amounts of food. His breakfast alone included three fried egg sandwiches, three chocolate pancakes, a five-egg omelette, toast, and oatmeal. Daily he aimed to eat 10,000 calories, five times more than the normal intake for a man.

Ian Thorpe, of Australia.

American swimmer Michael Phelps, the most successful Olympic competitor ever.

Amazing Olympics

Australia's Ian Thorpe, known as the "Thorpedo," has won five Olympic gold medals, the most won by any Australian.

Female Swimmers

Some of the most successful female Olympians are swimmers. American Jennifer Beth Thompson has the most swimming medals. She won 12 altogether, eight of them gold medals, between 1992 and 2000. She began her swimming training when she was seven years old. Another incredible Olympic achiever is American swimmer Natalie Coughlin, who won 11 medals, including three gold medals, in the 2004 and 2008 Olympics.

Kayak and Sailing Stars

One of the greatest women Olympians ever is Birgit Schmidt-Fischer, the kayak canoe champion. She won 12 Olympic medals, eight of them gold, competing in six Olympic Games between 1980 and 2004, first for East Germany and then for unified Germany. Meanwhile, out at sea, Danish sailor Paul Elvstrom is the Games' most successful sailor, with four gold medals. He competed in the Olympic Games over a period of 40 years, from 1948 to 1972.

⬤ Awesome German canoeist Birgit Schmidt-Fischer (above and top) won an amazing 12 Olympic medals, eight of them gold.

Olympic Facts and Stats

The fastest men's swimming records
50 m freestyle: 21.30 secs. 100 m freestyle: 47.05 secs.
100 m backstroke: 52.54 secs.
100 m breaststroke: 58.91 secs.
100 m butterfly: 50.58 secs.

The fastest women's swimming records
50 m freestyle: 24.06 secs. 100 m freestyle: 53.12 secs.
100 m backstroke: 58.77 secs.
100 m breaststroke: 1.05.17.
100 m butterfly: 56.61 secs.

CHAMPIONS

Some Olympic sports can only be won with pinpoint accuracy by firing guns or arrows at a target. These absorbing contests have produced some great individual champions and teams.

Archery

There are four Olympic individual and team archery events for men and women. Their arrows travel at about 150 mph (240 km/h) to a target that's the equivalent of three tennis courts away. Women are the outstanding archery Olympians. The South Korean women's team is one of the most successful teams in the entire history of the Olympics, with six consecutive gold medals. One of the best individual archers ever is Kim Soo-Nyung of South Korea, who won her first gold when she was just 17, and has four gold medals, a silver, and a bronze.

Shooting

There are 15 pistol and rifle shooting events at the Summer Olympics. Contestants fire a set number of shots at a target in a set time limit, and win their way through different rounds of their competition. The first perfect score ever recorded in international rifle shooting was achieved at the Olympics in 1936

◀ Archer Queenie Newall of Great Britain won gold at the 1908 London Olympics. She was 53 at the time—still the oldest female winner of a gold medal.

by Willy Røgeberg of Norway, and because it was a perfect 300 it can never be beaten.

Mixed Events

Women and men used to compete together in the same shooting competitions. The first woman to win an Olympic medal was American Margaret Murdock, who got a silver in a mixed event. Then, in 1992, Zhang Shan of China caused an Olympic sensation when she won gold against male competitors in the skeet, an event where contestants fire a rifle at clay disks shot into the air. She is the only woman ever to win a gold in a mixed Olympic event and, after 1992, Olympic women shooters were separated from men. One of the most successful sports shooters of all time is Serbian Jasna Sekaric, who has won five Olympic medals, among many other titles.

🔺 Serbian sports superstar Jasna Sekaric has won five gold medals in women's shooting.

Amazing Olympics

Pierre de Coubertin, founder of the modern Olympic Games, was a champion pistol-shooter, so he made sure that there were shooting events at the Games.

Olympic Facts and Stats

Most shooting medals: Carl Osburn, USA, with 11 (five gold, four silver, two bronze) —1912/1920/1924.

Most archery medals (men): Hubert van Innis, Belgium, with nine (six gold, three silver) —1900/1920.

Most archery medals (women): Kim Soo-Nyung, South Korea, with six (four gold, one silver, one bronze)—1988/1992/2000.

Some Olympic sports are scored by judges. These include gymnastics, diving, synchronized swimming, dressage, and boxing in the Summer Olympics, and figure skating in the Winter Olympics.

The most successful Olympic medalist is the Russian gymnast Larysa Latynina, who has won more medals than anyone, male or female, in any Olympic sport. Between 1956 and 1964, she collected an incredible 18 medals, nine of them gold. She put her achievements down to a difficult childhood, growing up after World War II. She said her hardships taught her to work hard for success:

"I learned a great truth in my difficult childhood. Good never comes on a silver platter, while talent is primarily perseverance and hard work."

▶ Russian gymnast Larysa Latynina, who won a record-breaking 18 Olympic medals, more than anyone in history.

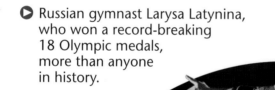

Amazing Olympics

Top medalists, including Larysa Latynina and Nadia Comãneci, are awarded a special honor—the Olympic Order—for their achievements.

Nadia Comăneci

Romanian gymnast Nadia Comăneci started doing gymnastics when she was six years old. When she was 12, she went to a school for gymnasts, where she trained for eight hours a day, six days a week. Her hard work led to a sensational performance in Montreal in 1976, when she became the first Olympic gymnast ever to score a perfect 10. Eventually she got seven perfect 10s at Montreal.

Figure Skating

Figure skating is one of the most popular sports at the Winter Olympics. The judges score the competitors for their artistic performance as well as for set moves. In 2002, Russian Alexei Yagudin set a record for the highest Olympic figure-skating score ever, with 106.6 points out of a possible 108. At Vancouver in 2010, 19-year-old South Korean Kim Yu-Na became the first female skater ever to get a combined score of more than 200 when she reached 228.56. At home, she is a superstar, nicknamed "Queen Yu-Na."

🔵 Kim Yu-Na of South Korea, the first female skater to achieve 200 points.

Olympic Facts and Stats

Most successful Olympic gymnast ever—Larysa Latynina (Russia)—18 medals (including nine gold).

Most successful male gymnast ever—Nikolai Andrianov (Russia)—15 medals (including seven golds).

Record gold medals in one day for any Olympic gymnast—Vitaly Scherbo (Russia) won a record four gold medals in one day at Barcelona in 1992.

Youngest gold medalist in the history of figure skating—Tara Lipinski (USA)—gold medal in figure skating age 15 in 1998.

RECORD-BREAKERS

The Summer and Winter Paralympics are for elite disabled athletes. They are held directly after the Summer and Winter Olympic Games, and they have led to many records and achievements.

The Paralympics are organized so that athletes with different disabilities compete in different events. This means that blind runners take part in separate events from runners with amputated limbs, for example. Some Paralympians have achieved incredible medal-winning success, none more so than Trischa Zorn of the USA. Blind from birth, she competed in Paralympic swimming events for the blind between 1980 and 2004 and won 55 medals, 41 of them Olympic gold.

Oscar Pistorius

South African Oscar Pistorius is the only Paralympian sprinter ever to hold Olympic records for the 100 m, 200 m, and 400 m sprints. He had both his legs amputated below the knee when he was one year old, and he wears flexible carbon-fiber "Cheetah Flex-Foot" blades to help him run. He is nicknamed "Blade Runner," and has broken many world records.

◀ South African Paralympic star Oscar Pistorius runs on carbon-fiber blades.

Ragnhild Myklebust

In a fantastically successful career between 1988 and 2002, Ragnhild Myklebust of Norway won 22 medals, 17 of them gold in the Winter Paralympics. She is a survivor of the disease polio, and used a custom-made lightweight chair mounted on skis to compete in cross-country and biathlon sit-skiing and ice-sled speed racing. She won her final gold medal at the age of 58, to become the most successful Winter Paralympian of all time.

Amazing Olympics

In 1984, Neroli Fairhall of New Zealand became the first person to compete in both the Paralympics and the Summer Olympics. She took part in archery contests.

⬤ Norwegian Ragnhild Myklebust won a record-breaking 22 Winter Paralympian medals in her lightweight ice-sled.

Olympic Facts and Stats

Clodoaldo Silva (Brazil), a male swimmer with cerebral palsy, won 11 Paralympic medals, six of them gold, between 2000–2004.

Between 1992 and 2004, Martina Willing (Germany), a blind female wheelchair-bound athlete, won ten Olympic medals, eight in Summer Paralympic field events and two in Winter Paralympic cross-country skiing.

Mayumi Narita (Japan), a wheelchair-bound swimmer, won 20 Paralympic medals, 15 of them gold, between 1996 and 2004.

Between 1988 and 2004, Dame Tanni Grey-Thompson (Great Britain) won 16 medals, 11 of them gold, as a wheelchair racer over distances between 100 m and 800 m.

The Winter Olympics have produced many great champions since they began in 1924, but speed and distance records are not kept for many events, because courses are different at each venue.

The most successful Winter Olympian of all time is Bjørn Daehlie, the Norwegian cross-country skier. He has 12 medals—eight gold and four silver—which he won in the 1990s. He would probably have won more but had to give up after a serious skiing accident. Instead, he went on to host his own TV show and become a millionaire businessman selling sportswear.

Speed Skating

Speed skating provides the fastest records in the Winter Olympics. Speed skaters race each other in time trials, powering over the ice at speeds up to 31 mph (50 km/h). German women's speed skater Claudia Pechstein is one of the most successful, with five gold medals, two silver, and a bronze. The shortest skating race—the 500 m—has an Olympic men's record of just 34.42 seconds, and the women's record is only three seconds behind. The longest winter Olympic distance records are held by the ski-jumpers.

▶ German speed skater Claudia Pechstein powers around the track on her way to winning another gold medal.

Swiss ski jumper Simon Ammann set a new benchmark in 2010 when he jumped a huge 472.44 feet (144 m). He now has four Olympic gold ski-jumping medals.

Snowboarding

Snowboarding became an Olympic sport in 1988, and has started producing medal-winning heroes. The most famous Olympic snowboarder of all is American Shaun White, the first double gold-medalist ever in snowboarding. He is nicknamed "The Flying Tomato" because of his long red hair.

▶ Olympic snowboarder Shaun White is now a multimillionaire global superstar.

Olympic Facts and Stats

Highest number of Winter Games medals won by women:
10—Raisa Smetanina (Russia)—cross-country skiing—1976–1992
10—Stefania Belmondo (Italy)—cross-country skiing—1992–2002
9—Lyubov Egorova (Russia)—cross-country—1992–2002
9—Uschi Disl (Germany)—biathlon (cross-country skiing and shooting)—1992–2006
9—Claudia Pechstein (Germany)—speed skating—1992–2006

Highest number of Winter Games medals won by men:
12—Bjørn Daehlie (Norway)—cross-country skiing—1992–1998
9—Ole Einar Bjoerndalen (Norway)—biathlon—1994–2006
9—Sixten Jernberg (Sweden)—cross-country skiing—1956–1964
8—Kjetil Andre Aamodt (Norway)—alpine skiing—1992–2006

GLOSSARY

Amateur athlete Someone who doesn't earn money from their sport, which is not their full-time job.

Barbell A bar that can have weighted plates fitted on either end, for weightlifters to raise up.

Biathlon An event that combines a cross-country skiing race with a shooting competition.

Bull's-eye The center of a shooting or archery target. Hitting the bull's-eye scores the highest number of points.

Decathlon An event that consists of ten different sports. Competitors build up a score as they take part in each one.

Doping Taking illegal drugs to get a better sports performance.

Field events Events that take place in the middle of the main Olympic Stadium, such as high jump and long jump.

Fosbury flop A type of backward high-jump technique.

Heptathlon An event that consists of seven sports.

IOC International Olympic Committee, the organization that runs the Olympic Games. It is headed by the President of the IOC.

Judges Experts who give scores to Olympic competitors in sports such as gymnastics and figure skating.

Long-distance running Endurance races such as the 5,000 and 10,000 m and the marathon.

Marathon A long-distance running race that takes place through the streets of the host city during the Summer Olympics.

Middle-distance running Races of 800 m, 1,500 m, and 3,000 m.

Modern pentathlon An event that consists of five different sports.

Olympian Someone who has competed in the Olympics.

Paralympics Summer and Winter Olympic Games held every four years for disabled athletes.

Performance-enhancing drugs Drugs taken to make an athlete perform better (also called "doping").

Photo-finish When two athletes finish so close together that judges have to study photos taken at the finish line, to decide on the winner.

Professional athlete Someone whose sport is their full-time job, from which they earn money.

Skeet A shooting event, where competitors fire at clay disks shot into the air.

Sprinter A fast runner who runs in short races of 100 m, 200 m, or 400 m.

Stadion The very first race run in the first ever ancient Olympics, a sprint of approximately 210 yards (192.2 m).

Synchronized A sport where a team must make exactly the same movements at the same time, such as synchronized swimming and diving.

Touchpads Electronic sensors built into the walls of the Olympic swimming pool, to record times when swimmers touch them.

Track events Athletics events that are run around the track in the main Olympic Stadium.

Trial An event competitors enter to qualify for the Olympics.

Modern Summer Olympic Games Timeline

1896 Athens, Greece

1900 Paris, France

1904 St. Louis, Missouri

1908 London, UK

1912 Stockholm, Sweden

1916 Canceled because of World War I

1920 Antwerp, Belgium

1924 Paris, France

1928 Amsterdam, Netherlands

1932 Los Angeles, California

1936 Berlin, Germany

1940 Canceled because of World War II

1944 Canceled because of World War II

1948 London, UK

1952 Helsinki, Finland

1956 Melbourne, Australia

1960 Rome, Italy (First Paralympic Summer Games also held)

1964 Tokyo, Japan

1968 Mexico City, Mexico

1972 Munich, West Germany

1976 Montreal, Canada

1980 Moscow, USSR

1984 Los Angeles, California

1988 Seoul, South Korea

1992 Barcelona, Spain

1996 Atlanta, Georgia

2000 Sydney, Australia

2004 Athens, Greece

2008 Beijing, China

2012 London, UK

2016 Rio de Janiero, Brazil

Winter Olympics Timeline

1924 Chamonix, France

1928 St. Moritz, Switzerland

1932 Lake Placid, New York

1936 Garmisch, Germany

1940 Canceled because of World War II

1944 Canceled because of World War II

1948 St. Moritz, Switzerland

1952 Oslo, Norway

1956 Cortina d'Ampezzo, Italy

1960 Squaw Valley, California

1964 Innsbruck, Austria

1968 Grenoble, France

1972 Sapporo, Japan

1976 Innsbruck, Austria

1976 First Paralympic Winter Games held Ornskoldsvik, Sweden

1980 Lake Placid, New York

1984 Sarajevo, Yugoslavia (now Bosnia)

1988 Calgary, Alberta, Canada

1992 Albertville, France

1994 Lillehammer, Norway

1998 Nagano, Japan

2002 Salt Lake City, Utah

2006 Turin, Italy

2010 Vancouver, British Colombia, Canada

Useful Olympic Web Sites

www. olympic.org The official web site of the Olympic Movement.

www.teamusa.org Official site for the U.S. Olympic Team.

www. london2012.com The official web site of the London Summer Olympics, 2012.

www.paralympics.org The official web site of the Paralympics.

http://www.historyforkids.org/learn/greeks/games/olympics.htm Find out about the history of the Ancient Greek Games.

INDEX